MY Confessions of FAITH

31-Days to Activate the Power of Your Words

by

SHAKIRA N. JONES

Watersprings
PUBLISHING

Published by Watersprings Publishing, a division of
Watersprings Media House, LLC.
P.O. BOX 1284
Olive Branch, MS 38654
www.waterspringsmedia.com
Contact publisher for bulk orders and permission requests.

Copyrights © 2020 by Shakira N. Jones

All rights reserved. No part of this publication may be reproduced, distributed, or transmitted in any form or by any means, including photocopying, recording, or other electronic or mechanical methods, without the prior written permission of the publisher, except in the case of brief quotations embodied in critical reviews and certain other noncommercial uses permitted by copyright law.

Scripture quotations marked (NLT) are taken from the Holy Bible, New Living Translation, copyright © 1996. Used by permission of Tyndale House Publishers, Inc., Wheaton, IL 60189 USA. All rights reserved.

Scripture quotations credited to NIV are from the Holy Bible, New International Version. Copyright © 1973, 1978, 1984, 2011 by Biblica, Inc. Used by permission. All rights reserved worldwide.

Scripture quotations marked "NKJV" are taken from the New King James Version. Copyright © 1982 by Thomas Nelson, Inc. Used by permission. All rights reserved.

Printed in the United States of America.

Library of Congress Control Number: 2020904357

ISBN-13: 978-1-948877-53-4

Table of Contents

	Introduction	7
Day 1	My Words Have Power	11
Day 2	I Am Grateful	14
Day 3	I Am An Influencer	17
Day 4	I Have Purpose	20
Day 5	I Am Free	23
Day 6	I Have More Than What I Need	26
Day 7	My Heart Is Whole	29
Day 8	I Am Living The Abundant Life	32
Day 9	My Faith Will Not Fail	35
Day 10	I Have Confidence	38
Day 11	I Am Amazing	41
Day 12	I Am Unrelenting	44
Day 13	I Relinquish Control	47
Day 14	I Am Enough	40
Day 15	I Am Not Alone	53
Day 16	I Am At Peace	56
Day 17	I Am Valuable	59
Day 18	I Have Hope	62
Day 19	I Am Ready For Overflow	65
Day 20	Fear Will Not Win	68
Day 21	God Provides For Me	71
Day 22	I Am Full Of Possibilities	74

Day 23	I Can Have Whatever I Say	77
Day 24	I Am Living My Best Life	80
Day 25	I Am A Culture Changer	83
Day 26	I'm Coming Back Strong	86
Day 27	I Am A Giant Slayer	89
Day 28	I Release It	92
Day 29	I Will Never Be Defeated	95
Day 30	I Am Loved	99
Day 31	My Future Awaits Me	101
	My Confessions Of Faith	105
	About The Author	108

This book is dedicated to
every dreamer and every visionary.
May your faith carry you and
manifest every gift, vision, and idea.

"Faith shows the reality of what we hope for;
it is the evidence of things we cannot see."

"By faith we understand that the entire universe was
formed at God's command, that what we now see did not
come from anything that can be seen."

Hebrews 11:1; 3 (NLT)

Introduction

Faith: believing without seeing; confidence; assurance

My *Confessions of Faith* is a series of declarative statements used to encourage, motivate, and inspire. Some people say affirmations, but we call them confessions of faith. Faith, in the simplest of terms is "believing without seeing." To confess something is to make a factual statement. By confessing our faith, we are making declarative statements of what we know to be true and speaking them into existence without seeing them. Friend, our words have power, and they frame our entire world. Although this book is full of declarative statements designed to motivate, it is so much more than that. My Confessions of Faith is an entire belief system; it is a way of life. It is the foundation upon which everything else is built.

In Genesis chapter 1 verse 1 the Bible begins to recount the creation story. In Genesis chapter 1 verse 3 to be exact, the Bible says:

> "Then God said, "Let there be light,"
> and there was light."

That's it, God said it, and it happened. Well, I believe that same power lies within us. We have the power to speak and cause what we have spoken to manifest. Now, please don't be fooled. None of us are God, so no one can say "let there be one million dollars" and *POOF* one million dollars suddenly appears! That's not exactly how it works. Instead, I can declare "I will have one million dollars" and believe in faith that I will actually have it. Once I have spoken it, then it is up to me to believe and then put some action behind what's been said.

> *"Just as the body is dead without breath, so also faith is dead without good works"*
> James 2:26 NLT

In January 2014, I was sitting at dinner with my then boyfriend, and we were discussing future plans. I knew I wasn't happy with our relationship, and I needed a change. I don't remember how we got on the subject, but somehow I blurted out, "I can see myself moving to Atlanta." Now, let me tell you, the thought of moving to Atlanta had not even crossed my mind (as an adult) but there it was. Later that evening as I sat in my bedroom in the Bronx, NY, I began the process of writing the vision. I wrote down where I wanted to move, when I wanted to move, what kind of job, salary, car, and home I wanted. I wrote it ALL, I prayed and then I started putting some work behind it. I searched for jobs in Atlanta but nothing worked out so after a few months I stopped.

Fast forward to July 2014, I was no longer in that relationship, and I was let go from my job. After the initial shock wore off, I was CRUSHED! I was unemployed and had too many responsibilities for life to remain that way! A short time later, I went on my planned trip to visit my best friend in Charleston, SC. I remember sitting on her couch crying because I was unemployed and needed money. After I cried, I pulled out the laptop and began searching for jobs in Atlanta. I sent out a few resumes and left it alone.

When I returned home to NY, I had an email from one job in particular requesting me to come in for an interview that week. I was about to go out of town again that weekend for my church's youth retreat. I was one of the leaders, so there was no way I could make it. The employer agreed to allow me to interview the following week. I returned home on a Saturday evening (August 2, 2014), flew to Atlanta the following day, interviewed Monday, August 4, 2014, and had a second interview on Friday, August 8, 2014. On August 12, 2014, I was officially offered the job. Six days later on Monday, August 18, 2014, I boarded a one-way flight bound for Atlanta.

As a result, the past five years have been full of confession after confession and manifestation. Confessing what you want, confessing your faith (what you are believing for) is the foundation to getting everything you've ever wanted! There is something so powerful about writing things down and speaking it out of your mouth that makes the "idea" so real and very tangible.

Why don't you give it a try?!?! Say what you want, do the work and watch it manifest in time. Use the final pages in this book to write your additional daily confessions of faith.

My Words Have Power

*"The tongue can bring death or life;
those who love to talk will reap the consequences."*
Proverbs 18:21 (NLT)

The concept is really simple; you want it, you say it! Many of us fail to realize that our entire world is framed by the words that we speak. Think about it, God created the entire world, the galaxies, stars, planets, seas, plants, animals. He created them all with His words. God spoke it, and it was so! God said _____, and it was so. If God can speak things into existence, and we are His children, that means that we have this same power.

What are the things you want to see in your lifetime? What are your hopes? What are your dreams? What visions has God given you? If you want to see all of these things made a reality in your life, you have to start confessing it. Confession has a way of breeding motivation and motivation eventually births action. Once you confess it out of your mouth, take the necessary steps to make that dream a reality. You may not see it right now, but I promise you it will come.

Confess With Me:

- The words I speak have the ability to change the atmosphere around me.
- The words I speak paint a picture of what I am expecting.
- The words I speak heal others and myself.
- The words I speak have the power to change lives.

Thoughts:

I Am Grateful

*"Be thankful in all circumstances,
for this is God's will for you who belong to Christ Jesus."*
1 Thessalonians 5:18 (NLT)

What does it mean to be grateful? The dictionary defines the word grateful as feeling or showing an appreciation of kindness; thankful. The dictionary also tells us that in terms of grammar. The word grateful is an adjective, which means it is used to describe a noun (person, place, or thing). What an awesome descriptor to have! Think about it, if someone asks you, "Oh what do you know about Jasmine?" The response is, "she's such a grateful person." I don't know about you but I'd love to be described as being grateful, a person who is appreciative when something is done for me.

The fact of the matter is, sometimes life is rough, and it can be hard to maintain a grateful heart. We can become consumed by the "Lord why?" Our questioning can then turn to complaints when things just don't seem to be going our way. What would happen if, instead of questioning God or complaining we simply said, "Thank You"? What would that do to our perspective? How could a simple thank you change our world? My childhood pastor would always tell us that "thank you" makes room for more! Let's think about it for a moment, when you do something for someone, and they say thank you, how does it make you feel? Are you more or less likely to bless that person again? Now, think about how the Lord feels when we show our appreciation for the many things He's done for us!

The Bible tells us that we should give thanks in EVERY situation because this is what God wants for us. The abundance that you are seeking begins with a grateful heart. I promise if you change your perspective, your entire world will begin to shift.

Confess With Me:

- My perspective is changing.
- I choose to be grateful for what I have.
- I choose not to focus on lack.
- I choose to be satisfied and content.
- My grateful attitude will make room for abundance.

Thoughts:

I Am An Influencer

"And who knows whether you have attained royalty for such a time as this [and for this very purpose]?"

Esther 4:14b (AMP)

Influencer: someone who has the capacity to have an effect on the character, development, or behavior of someone or something.

Let's take a look at Queen Esther, who unbeknownst to her, was chosen by God to deliver her people, the Jews. Esther was an orphan being raised by an older cousin and was summoned to the king's palace based on her beauty after a decree went out. Esther was favored by the king and was named the new queen. Because of the king's love for her, Esther was able to request what she wanted and it was granted. After learning of one of the king's officials had plans to annihilate the Jews, Esther went to the king and requested that her people be saved. Ultimately the Jews were saved and given the authority to defend themselves and kill anyone who came after them.

Esther had so much influence with the king that all she needed to do was make a simple request and her request was granted. She believed in her ability and in her God. As a result, she faced the king with confidence.

What are the areas in your life where you seek to have influence? Where do you wish to see changes being made? Just like Esther had favor with the king, you my friend have favor with the King of all kings. If you belong to Christ you can go boldly to Him and ask for whatever you will. You have the power and the authority to invoke change simply because of who you are and who you are connected to. Your request has the ability to save a nation and change the course of history.

Confess With Me:

- My words are powerful.
- My words have influence.
- My words shift cultures.
- My words bring about change.

Thoughts:

DAY 4
I Have Purpose

"For I know the plans I have for you," says the Lord. "They are plans for good and not for disaster, to give you a future and a hope."

Jeremiah 29:11 (NLT)

In 2017, the Earth's population was an estimated 7.53 billion people! In the grand scheme of things, that is A LOT of people! But with all the billions of people on this planet, there is only one you. Even if you are a twin, a triplet, or even a quadruplet, there is still no one in this world quite like you.

I remember a time when I felt super inadequate. Others would look at me and see my accomplishments, but on the inside, I was quite insecure and unsure of myself. I felt like God was calling me to do great things, but I would begin to look around at others doing the very thing I felt I was supposed to be doing and I would become discouraged. I battled with self-doubt, negative self-talk, procrastination and so much more. I knew there was something special about me. Then again, I wasn't sure if I really believed that. Once I started making confessions, I had to ask myself if I really believed the things I was saying. God had to remind me that I was created in His mind for a specific purpose, a purpose that could only be filled by me. You, my friend, were created for a purpose, one that can only be filled by YOU.

You may be thinking, "Well I don't know my purpose," or "what am I here for?" My friend, you are not alone. Everyone, at one time or another, has asked those very same questions. "What am I supposed to be doing with my life? What am I here for?" It may take some time to uncover, but it is actually very simple to figure it out (at least in part). Think about it for a moment, what are you good at? What are your passions? What is it that you feel drawn or called to? Now that you have those things in mind, take it to God in prayer. After all, He is the one who causes us to have these ideas, these passions, and abilities. It is God who has the ultimate plan for our lives. He knows the purpose for which He's created you, and if you get connected to Him, He is sure to reveal it to you.

You are important. You are loved. Your gift is necessary, and there is no one else who can do it quite like you can. You have purpose, and the world is awaiting its fulfillment.

Confess With Me:

- I have purpose.
- My life is not solely my own.
- God knows the plans He has for my life.
- The lives of others is awaiting my purpose to be fulfilled.
- Every step I take brings me one step closer to fulfilling my purpose.

Thoughts:

I Am Free

"For you have been called to live in freedom."
Galatians 5:13a (NLT)

Free: not under the control or the power of another; able to act or be done as one wishes; not or no longer confined or imprisoned.

Freedom! What an amazing gift that many of us don't realize we are missing out on. Life is filled with ups and downs, highs and lows, twists and turns, and sometimes we become so caught up and entangled in life that it feels as though we are suffocating. Maybe it starts off as a small seed of self-doubt, that small thought that creeps into your mind to remind you about how you failed the last time so you can't possibly be successful this time. Then before you know it, that small seed has grown into this giant tree with a mass of branches that are literally choking the life (and the dreams) out of you. You fight and fight until you're just too tired to fight anymore, and ultimately you just accept life for what it is, one giant pile of mess trying to take you out. What if I told you that you don't have to live that way? What if I told you that freedom is available? What if I told you that freedom is as close as your mouth?

Sure freedom is a process that takes time, but it begins with *believing* that you can actually be free. Once you believe it you have to confess it. Begin to confess to yourself that everything holding you back no longer has power or control over you. You may feel weak or helpless, but the fact of the matter is that you don't have to succumb to the pressures of life. Life is TOUGH and it can throw some really hard blows, but it can only take you out if you allow it to. My friend, I invite you to go get your life back and join me in experiencing true freedom.

Confess With Me:

- I am free from my past.
- I am free from self-doubt.
- I am free from insecurities.
- I am free to go after all God has for me.

Thoughts:

I Have More Than What I Need

"Give, and you will receive. Your gift will return to you in full—pressed down, shaken together to make room for more, running over, and poured into your lap. The amount you give will determine the amount you get back."

Luke 6:38 (NLT)

"I give because I have; I have because I give. Therefore, I am never without."

Author unknown

I remember growing up. The church across the street from mine had this quote on the side of the building, and I never really understood it until I was a little older. I now understand the more I give of myself, my time, resources and abilities, the more God causes others to give to me.

Often times we sit around and talk about what we don't have. Quite frankly, it's easy to talk about what's not, but it can be difficult to turn that around to make it a positive. I challenge you today to change your confession. Instead of complaining about what has not happened or what you don't have, begin to confess the opposite. Don't know where to start? Use the Word of God as your roadmap. The Bible says you are the head and not the tail, above only and never beneath, a lender to the nations and no longer a borrower. My friend, the key to having more than what you need is in your mouth. Change your confession today, and watch your mind and your entire world shift.

Confess With Me:
- All of my needs are met.
- God always provides for me.
- I am generous with what I have.
- I am a good steward over my possessions.

Thoughts:

DAY 7

My Heart Is Whole

*"Guard your heart above all else,
for it determines the course of your life."*

Proverbs 4:23 (NLT)

The heart is a vital yet fragile organ. It is the source of our life, yet it is often also the source of pain. Disappointment and upset have crept in and made themselves at home in your heart. As a result, you've become closed off and cold without even realizing it. You are protecting your heart because you can't bear the thought of being hurt again. I'm pretty sure everyone reading this has felt that way at some point in time. I know what it's like to want to protect yourself, but I also know what it's like to allow my heart to heal and be made whole.

May I suggest to you that heartache is a part of our life's process. It teaches us and molds us in a way that no other experience can. It is through disappointment and hurt that we learn how strong we are. It is through the storms of life that we learn what we are made of. It is through the mud and the disgusting parts of life that we have the opportunity to really learn who God is. Yes, you've been hurt, you've been disappointed, life has thrown you some devastating blows, and your heart has been broken into a million pieces, but you don't have to stay in that place. You can have a whole and complete heart again if you open up and allow our great and loving Father to begin to put the pieces back together again.

Confess With Me:
- I am free to love.
- I am free to forgive.
- I will not allow the mistreatment from others to break me.
- My heart is healed and whole, and I am free.

Thoughts:

DAY 8
I Am Living The Abundant Life

"A thief is only there to steal and kill and destroy. I came so they can have real and eternal life, more and better life than they ever dreamed of."

John 10:10 (MSG)

You want better? Start confessing it! The Bible tells us above that Christ came to give us an abundant life, but what does abundant even mean?

Abundant: available in large quantities; plentiful.

I don't know about you, but this is the kind of life I want to live! I don't want just enough. I want overflow. I want large quantities, more than enough. I want the abundant life! Now, I'm not just referring to monetary abundance either. I'm talking about abundance in my personal life, professional life, my health, my businesses and everything else that pertains to me. I want the kind of life that Jesus described in John 10:10. I want to have a life that's better than anything I've ever dreamed of.

What does an abundant life mean to you? Is it traveling? Is it being surrounded by friends and other loved ones? Does it mean enjoying every moment you've been given despite the challenges? Whatever the abundant life looks like for you, just know that you can have it. Confess with your mouth, believe in your heart, make a plan and put it in action. You, my friend, can have the abundant life you're seeking.

Confess With Me:
- I am a lender, never a borrower.
- I have more than enough.
- I am generous.
- I live in overflow.
- I am grateful for where I am and what I have, but I am looking ahead.

Thoughts:

My Faith Will Not Fail

"But I have pleaded in prayer for you, Simon, that your faith should not fail. So when you have repented and turned to me again, strengthen your brothers."

Luke 22:32 (NLT)

Today, I confess that my faith will NOT fail! Let's be honest, sometimes it's really hard to believe when everything around you is pointing in the opposite direction of what you need or what you want. If you ask me, having faith is a conscious decision, and it takes determination. The good thing, however, is that the Bible tells us that we only need to have faith the size of a mustard seed. Have you ever seen a mustard seed? If not, take a moment and google a picture of it. It's a rather small seed that packs a powerful punch! Jesus tells us in Matthew chapter 17 verse 20, "If we have faith the size of a mustard seed, we can tell a mountain to move from here to there (metaphorically speaking). Mountains are rather LARGE. That must mean your faith packs A LOT of power!

My friend, if you only believe, there are so many wonderful things that you will begin to unlock in your lifetime. Remember, faith without some action behind it is dead (James 2:17), so couple your faith with your deeds and watch miraculous things unfold! Don't let your faith fail you. Believe in God, believe in yourself, and go after every desire!

Confess With Me:
- My faith will not fail.
- I may not see it, but I believe it.
- My faith is stronger than my fear.
- Every day I confess my desires will be manifested in the earth.

Thoughts:

DAY 10
I Have Confidence

"Being confident of this very thing, that He who has begun a good work in you will complete it."
Philippians 1:6 (NKJV)

Confidence: the feeling or belief that one can rely on someone or something; firm trust; a feeling of self-assurance arising from one's appreciation of one's own abilities or qualities.

Have you ever struggled with feeling confident or believing in yourself? I know I sure have! There have been so many times when I have looked in the mirror and scrutinized every single thing I saw. I've criticized myself, talked down to myself, compared myself to other women, thinking oh if only I looked this way, or if only I had made that move back then. I've doubted my God-given abilities and the wonderful gifts and ideas He's given me.

Let's take this book for instance. God began planting the seeds for this book back in 2015/2016. I used to be a habitual goal setter too, writing down all the visions and dreams God gave me but never taking any real action towards making them a reality. I would look at what others were doing via social media and begin to compare myself to them. My confidence and my fire dwindled, and I was full of doubt. Then one day in 2019 something just clicked! Despite what I thought about myself, I came to realize that I already possessed everything I needed to cause every dream and idea to come to life. I was reminded of the words of Paul in Philippians chapter 1 verse 6 that the One (God) who started this good work in me back in 2015/2016 was and is able to complete it. I had to take some time to talk to myself and remind myself of who I am and who I belong to.

My friend, you are going to have moments of doubt because that's just life, and it's human nature. But I'm telling you, if you just begin to take small steps by confessing your faith and believing in the Creator who has blessed you with these visions and ideas, there is nothing that will stop you. You may struggle to believe. You may struggle to see the beauty and the greatness that's in front of you. Trust me when I tell you that getting to that place where you finally see is beautiful. Today, I want you to be confident in the God inside of you. He is there to help you, push you, lift you, and guide you on your journey. Have confidence in Him and His supernatural ability to get you to the next level.

Confess With Me:

- Today, I will exercise confidence in who I am and all of my abilities.
- I believe that God has granted me wisdom and skill in all that I do.
- I am confident in the One who has created me.

Thoughts:

DAY 11
I Am Amazing

"You made all the delicate, inner parts of my body and knit them together in my mother's womb. Thank you for making me so wonderfully complex! It is amazing to think about. Your workmanship is marvelous—and how well I know it."

Psalm 139:13-14 (The Living Bible)

I AM AMAZING! Now that may sound a bit arrogant or conceited to some but it's really not. It's a positive self-statement that evokes confidence. When you truly realize just how wonderfully unique you are, you develop a sense of pride where you no longer feel the need to compare yourself or your journey to the next person. You in your flawed human state were hand selected by God to be here. You alone were gifted with certain skills and abilities that no one else can quite execute the way that you can. The Bible tells us that we are *fearfully* and wonderfully made. The word "fearfully" in that scripture means to cause astonishment or to be held in awe. God created you so that you would be held in awe or amazement.

My friend, today, I encourage you to take a look at yourself and view yourself in the same way that our loving heavenly

Father does. Search scriptures and learn what God has to say about you. You are a masterpiece, flaws, setbacks, mishaps and all. You were perfectly handcrafted by the Creator of the universe to be exactly who you are.

Confess With Me:

- I was uniquely created.
- I have skills and abilities that are unique to me.
- I am exactly where I am supposed to be in my life's journey.
- I appreciate and accept myself for being who I am without apology.
- I am amazing, and I do not have to compare myself or my journey to anyone else.

Thoughts:

I Am Unrelenting

"I have not achieved it, but I focus on one thing: Forgetting the past and looking forward to what lies ahead, I press on to reach the end of the race."

Philippians 3:13-14 (NLT)

Unrelenting: not yielding in strength, severity, or determination.

In the book of Philippians, the Apostle Paul likened the Christian lifestyle to running a race. He talked about not attaining the prize yet but still moving forward to reach the prize at the end of the race. Maybe you've experienced some setbacks. Maybe things haven't gone as planned. Your kids may be out of control, business ideas may not be gaining the momentum you thought, no advancement in your career, stagnant in your health. The list could go on and on. Reality says that we all experience setbacks in life but the difference comes in when we choose not to give up. Today, my friend I challenge you to forget about the past. Forget about the hurts, losses, disappointments, and anything else that will try to hold you back. Today, I pray that you develop a fight and a determination on the inside that does not allow you to quit, give up, pause or shrink back. I pray for strength of will and that you develop a determination that causes you to move forward in the face of setbacks and adversity.

Confess With Me:
- I am determined.
- I never give up.
- I go after what I want with fervor, confidence and skill.
- I have the wisdom to work smarter not harder.

Thoughts:

I Relinquish Control

"Trust in the Lord with all your heart; do not depend on your own understanding."

Proverbs 3:5 (NLT)

I know that many people reading this book can identify with the feeling of needing to be in control of every aspect of your life. Control can look different for each of us too. For one person, it may be always wanting to know what's coming next. For someone else, control may include a lack of trust and wanting to do everything without help. As humans, we are flawed and prone to error. Naturally speaking, it is not easy to give up control and put your trust in someone else to make sure you're okay or that things are taken care of. Don't you know, the more you try to hold on to control the more likely you are to be stressed?

Today, my friend, I challenge you to place your faith and trust in God. If you want to experience peace, allow Him to take the reins; allow Him to be the captain of the ship who guides you on your way and leads you to safety. Accept help when it's offered, knowing it takes a strong person to admit when they are unable to do it all on their own. Give yourself some grace today. Remember, you don't have to have all the answers, God is big enough to handle it, and He's just waiting for you to accept the help He is offering.

Confess With Me:
- Today, I am accepting of help.
- Today, I am choosing to rely on God.
- Today, I let go of my need to do it all myself.
- Today, I understand that God sends people to help with what I cannot accomplish alone.

Thoughts:

I Am Enough

*"So God created human beings in his own image.
In the image of God he created them;
male and female he created them."*

Genesis 1:27 (NLT)

Have you ever felt small? Insignificant? Not good enough? I know I surely have! I spent time diminishing the great things about myself simply because I didn't think I was good enough. Or because I felt that others were better suited or better equipped to do the things I wanted to do. Once I realized that I was created in the image of God, my mindset and my world began to change. I mean, come on, it gets no better than God, the Creator of the universe Himself. The Almighty, all powerful, all knowing King of all. God created me in HIS image and in HIS likeness so that HAS to count for something! If for no other reason, I know that I am enough simply because I have been created in the image of my heavenly Father and there is absolutely no error in Him, which means that there is no error in me.

My friend, I want you to take a moment and remind yourself that you are God's special gift to this world. There is no one quite like you, and no one can bring to the table the things that you have to offer. You (and everything that comes along with you) are enough. No need to try to become something or someone you are not. You, in all of your uniqueness and authenticity are indeed ENOUGH.

Confess With Me:
- I am smart enough.
- I'm not perfect but I am good enough.
- I don't need to become who and what I'm not.
- I don't need to shrink in order for someone else to be great.

Thoughts:

I Am Not Alone

"So be strong and courageous! Do not be afraid and do not panic before them. For the Lord your God will personally go ahead of you. He will neither fail you nor abandon you."

Deuteronomy 31:6 (NLT)

Alone: having no one else present; on one's own

One of the greatest challenges that many of us face is the feeling of being alone, feeling as if you have no one, or no one cares. Feeling as though you have no help and you have to figure out life on your own. Honey, that ain't nothing but a cheap trick and a straight up lie! As a Christian, I believe that the enemy (Satan) wants us to feel that way. He wants us to feel all alone because as humans that is when we are at our weakest point. Think about it, the politician with the most votes wins the election, or the game at recess with the most votes will be played (Can you tell I work with kids?). The point is that there is power in numbers! The feeling of being alone leaves you feeling powerless, weak, and defeated. My friend, I want to encourage you that even when you feel alone, you are not alone. You are loved, you are important, and you are cared for. Even when people are not around, know that you're heavenly Father is right there beside you and will never leave your side. Today, do yourself a favor and begin to reject and renounce those thoughts that tell you that you're alone and uncared for.

Confess With Me:

- I am loved.
- I am cared for.
- I am supported.
- I do not have to do life on my own.

Thoughts:

I Am At Peace

Don't worry about anything; instead, pray about everything. Tell God what you need, and thank him for all he has done. Then you will experience God's peace, which exceeds anything we can understand. His peace will guard your hearts and minds as you live in Christ Jesus.

Philippians 4:6-7 (NLT)

As I sit here writing, I'm reminded of an old song I learned in church in my youth…

"Be not dismayed whate'er be 'tied, God will take care of you. Beneath His wings of love abide, God will take care of you. I know God will take care of you, through every day, come what may He'll see you through. God will take care of you…" (God Will Take Care of You, Edwin Hawkins)

As an adult, and in this very moment, those words have brought me major comfort. No matter what may be going on in my life, I can rest assured that God will take care of me. Now, don't get it twisted, life is TOUGH and sometimes there are twists and turns, curveballs and straight up cliffhangers that leave us feeling anxious, bewildered, and completely out of sorts. It's totally normal to feel all of those things and more because you're human. However, here's where your confessions come in. Although life is tough and knocks you for a loop at times, your confessions, and your faith have to be tougher and stronger than that. My friend, your words are powerful beyond belief and you truly can have whatever you say.

There's a story in the Bible where Jesus was on a boat with His disciples and went to sleep. As Jesus was sleeping, a storm suddenly arose on the water and the disciples began to panic. They awakened Jesus and started shouting "Lord save us! We're going to drown!" Jesus calmly responded and said, "Why are you afraid? You have so little faith!" After that, He spoke to the winds and waves, "Peace, be still!" Then a calm came over the waters.

My friend, this is the God we serve today! The same power that is in Christ lies on the inside of you. He has the ability to calm any storm in your life. He has the ability to bring peace that can't be explained in the midst of the storm. Today, exercise that same power and command your storm, your mind, your body, and your soul to be at peace.

Confess With Me:
- Today, I am not moved by what I see.
- Today, I make a conscious decision to remain calm.
- Today, I will control only what I can and leave the rest alone.

Thoughts:

I Am Valuable

"...she is more precious than rubies..."
Proverbs 31:10 (NLT)

Valuable: a thing that is of great worth.

Have you ever felt worthless? Ever felt incomplete or as though you were lacking in something? You may have felt this way due to circumstances, mistakes, environment, or even harsh words from others and sometimes there's nothing we can do about any of those things. However, as you grow and mature, it's up to you to begin changing the narrative. Look on the inside and identify those special qualities you possess.

The Bible describes a woman in Proverbs 31 saying that her value is beyond that of rubies. If you know anything about rubies, you know that they are rare and costly, ranging from $10,000-$18,000 per carat. You possess so much greatness and so much value that it cannot be confined to where, what, or who you are now. My friend once your mindset shifts there is no stopping you. Sure, things may be crazy right now, but you have the power in your mouth to change the narrative. I challenge you to see yourself as being more precious, more important, more valuable than anything you see right now. Today, be reminded that God doesn't make mistakes. You were created for a reason and your life; your very being has value.

Confess With Me:
- I am worthy.
- I add value to any space I'm in.
- I possess greatness on the inside.
- I am more than what I see.

Thoughts:

I Have Hope

*"Why am I discouraged? Why is my heart so sad?
I will put my hope in God! I will praise him again,
my Savior and my God."*

Psalm 42:11 (NLT)

Hope: a feeling of expectation and desire for a certain thing to happen.

I don't know about you, but there have been several moments in my life where I've felt as though all hope was lost. I felt as though I was forgotten by God, and I questioned if certain things would ever happen for me the way I dreamt of them. One day in particular, I felt down about a situation where I was really looking for God to move on my behalf, and I started to become frustrated with the process. That night, I received a text message from someone about a dream they had concerning me and the very thing I had grown frustrated about. We chatted a bit, and I left the conversation feeling encouraged. The next morning a particular scripture that kept coming to mind over the preceding weeks returned:

Psalm 91:2 (NLT)

This I declare about the LORD:
He alone is my refuge, my place of safety;
He is my God, and I trust Him.

For some reason, the word *refuge* stood out more, so I looked it up and found out that part of the word refuge in this context means hope and trust. Then, I heard God say "hope," so I looked it up. The word *hope* in the Hebrew language means to wait, to be patient, to stay, to tarry, to trust. In that moment, God showed me all I had to do was put my hope in Him and trust His plan.

My friend, I don't know what you may be facing or what you may be waiting on, but I want to encourage you to "hope in God." Put your complete and total trust in Him, knowing that ultimately His plan is the best plan. I'm still waiting, but every day I choose to remind myself that I have hope, and it is in God.

Confess With Me:

- I am not forgotten.
- I am loved by God.
- I have hope.

Thoughts:

I Am Ready For Overflow

*"...Well done, my good and faithful servant;
You have been faithful over a few things,
I will make you ruler over many things..."*

Matthew 25:23 (NLT)

Today, I confess I am ready for overflow. Some years ago, I began making this confession, and while in and of itself, there's nothing wrong with it, I was reminded of something. In order to be ready for overflow, I must prepare for it. I must first use what has already been given to me and show I have the ability to handle more and handle it well.

In the Bible, Matthew records a story where Jesus shares a parable about a master and his servants. The master gives each servant a certain amount of money and goes away. Two of the three servants take what was given and used it for good and brought back the master more than what they had been given. The third servant however did nothing with what he was given and returned to the master only with what he was originally given. In Matthew 25:23, the Bible states the master blessed the servants who multiplied what they had been given by saying, "Well done, my good and faithful servant; You have been faithful over a few things, I will make you ruler over many things…" but to the servant who did nothing with what he was given, the master cursed him and called him lazy. The parable ends with the master saying, "To those who use well what they are given, even more will be given, and they will have an abundance. But from those who do nothing, even what little they have will be taken away." (Matthew 25:23 NLT).

I'd like to leave you with this thought: "If you want overflow in your life, how well are you managing what you already have?"

Confess With Me:

- I can be trusted with more.
- I am a good manager of what I already have.
- I am diligent in making room for overflow in my life.

Thoughts:

Fear Will Not Win

"For God has not given us a spirit of fear and timidity, but of power, love, and self-discipline."
2 Timothy 1:7 (NLT)

Fear is perhaps one of life's biggest dream killers. It's a monster that tells people what they can't do, cripples them and stops them from acting or moving forward. There have been several moments in my life where fear has stopped me from doing many things, including writing this book. Fear caused me to doubt myself and my abilities. It caused me to second guess the things I knew I was not just capable of doing, but also destined to do. In the midst of the fear and uncertainty, God used people to unknowingly encourage and push me. God started talking to me and reminded me to say what He said about me. As I started listening to God, I was reminded that fear does not come from God and that He has given me a spirit of power, love and self-discipline.

What has fear stolen from you? What are the most intimate desires of your heart that you've allowed to lie dormant because of fear? My friend, it's time to go get your life back! Fear is a natural human emotion, but you cannot allow it to stop you from living your best life. Begin to build yourself up and confess God's Word over your life every day. Whatever is in your heart, you are more than capable to accomplish it with God on your side. Take a moment, take a deep breath and move in faith, not fear.

Confess With Me:
- Today, I denounce and reject fear.
- Today, I will move in faith, not fear.
- Today, I will say no to fear and yes to my destiny.

Thoughts:

God Provides For Me

"And if God cares so wonderfully for wildflowers that are here today and thrown into the fire tomorrow, he will certainly care for you. Why do you have so little faith?"

Matthew 6:30 (NLT)

Provide: make adequate preparation for; to supply.

Today, I want to encourage you to place your trust in God. So many times we as humans put all of our time and energy into trying to figure it all out or trying to make ends meet, and honestly it can become very overwhelming. From financial stress to mental health and emotional wellness. We are multifaceted beings and there are many areas in our lives where provision is needed. One person may need peace of mind while another person needs to be presented with the right opportunity to help launch that business idea. Yet, another person may need a little extra money to help make ends meet. Whatever it is that you stand in need of today, the formula is actually quite simple. I'll share with you something my childhood pastor would always say, "The key to answered prayer is the grace of God coupled with your self-effort.

Grace of God + Self Effort = Answered Prayer

Simple, if we do our part, God will certainly take care of the rest. If you're struggling financially, start by taking inventory of where your money is going. Create a budget and leave the rest up to God. If you're struggling emotionally, start by digging deep inside of yourself and getting to the root of the matter, acknowledge your pain, go see a therapist if needed and leave the rest in God's hands. If you need help getting that business off the ground, prepare yourself by creating a business plan and educating yourself on the business you are choosing to venture into. Then, take all of that, all of your self-effort and present it to God so that He can make a masterpiece of it all.

The bottom line my friend is that God is more than willing and able to take care of you. Are you willing to do your part?

Confess With Me:
- God provides for me.
- All of my needs are met.
- I will not worry about the future.
- I will do my part and allow God to do His.

Thoughts:

I Am Full Of Possibilities

"For I can do everything through Christ, who gives me strength."

Philippians 4:13 (NLT)

Self-doubt is one of the greatest barriers to a person realizing their full potential: questioning if you can actually go after your dreams, questioning if you have what it takes, and eventually convincing yourself it's better or safer to stay where you are, in your place of comfort. Let me tell you, that is no life to live! What are your dreams? What are your passions? What excites you? Whatever your "thing" is, go after it with full confidence and assurance. You don't have to stay stuck where you are my friend. Today, I want you to change your perspective. Instead of saying what you cannot do and talking about what looks impossible, start confessing what you CAN do. The possibilities for your life are endless. God has a plan for your life, and you have a purpose to fulfill. No more head in the sand. Today, we stand tall. Today, we affirm ourselves. Today, we let the world know that as long as there is breath in our lungs, the possibilities are endless, and we are unstoppable.

Confess With Me:

- I can do anything I set my mind to.
- My life is full of purpose.
- I am full of creative ideas.
- I have tenacity.
- I have perseverance.
- I will go, I will conquer.

Thoughts:

My Confessions Of Faith | 77

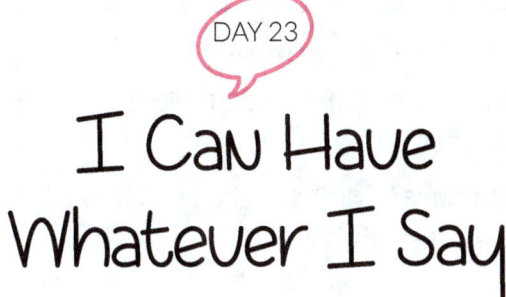

I Can Have Whatever I Say

"The tongue can bring death or life; those who love to talk will reap the consequences."
Proverbs 18:21 (NLT)

Food For Thought: What's coming out of your mouth?

The Bible tells us in Proverbs chapter 18 verse 21 that our tongue (mouth) is powerful, and it can bring death or life. In essence, it is our words that frame our world and cause things to come into existence. Be careful of the words you speak and purpose to only speak things that are going to be edifying, uplifting, and full of life. Even if the things around you don't look so good, never stop confessing.

    My friend, the bottom line is, you can, and WILL have whatever you say!

Feeling sick? Confess: by His stripes, I am already healed (Isaiah 53:5)

Money acting up? Confess: My God will supply ALL my needs according to His riches in glory (Philippians 4:19)

Low self-esteem? Confess: I will praise you, for I am fearfully and wonderfully made (Psalm 139:14)

Need direction? Confess: If I acknowledge God, He will direct my path (Proverbs 3:6)

Searching for peace? Confess: If I trust in God, He will keep me in perfect peace (Isaiah 26:3)

Confess With Me:
- If I think it, I can do it.
- If I speak it, I make it real.
- If I do the work, it will manifest.

Thoughts:

DAY 24
I Am Living My Best Life

"The thief's purpose is to steal and kill and destroy. My purpose is to give them a rich and satisfying life."

John 10:10 (NLT)

I'm living my best life is a phrase that has become very popular these days, but what does that even mean? Take a moment to actually think about what YOUR best life looks like? What are the things that make up your best life? Who are the people involved? Where are the places your best life will take you? Once you've visualized it, write it down. Be intentional, make a plan and begin doing the work necessary to create the best life you can possibly have. For some that may be going back to school, for others it may be finding a new job, starting a new business, traveling the world, or opening your heart to love again. My friend, whatever your personal best life may be, you have the power to go forth and create it. Don't allow anyone or anything to stop you from living the best, most abundant, fruitful and free life ever. You owe it to yourself to go after everything you want. You owe it to yourself to pursue every passion and every dream. Jesus said it himself; he came to give us a rich and satisfying life, so go on, go get your life!

Confess With Me:
- I am armed with purpose, vision, and my faith.
- I am dedicated to becoming the best version of myself.
- I will let no one and no thing stop me from living life to the fullest.
- I purpose to enjoy every moment of my journey.

Thoughts:

I Am A Culture Changer

"The thief's purpose is to steal and kill and destroy. My purpose is to give them a rich and satisfying life."
John 10:10 (NLT)

Have you ever questioned what your purpose is? Why was I born? What's the point? I'm sure at some point in life everyone reading this has pondered some of those very questions. Whether it be pertaining to a specific physical space you're in, or a general statement about your life as a whole; we all wonder about our purpose. Can I suggest to you that your purpose is to be a culture changer. You were placed on this earth to do something unique, a void and a purpose that can only be filled by you. You my friend are a culture changer!

What is a *culture changer*? A culture changer is someone who makes a shift in the world around them. A culture changer brings new, fresh, and innovative ideas to the table. Culture changers challenge the status quo and don't simply accept things as they are. Now ask yourself, what culture am I called to change? Who am I called to inspire? How can my passions and my purpose connect to create the change I wish to see in the culture around me?

Take time today to seek God in prayer. Ask Him to lead you and direct you on this journey. As you spend time with Him, He will begin to reveal to you all the ways you have already started changing the culture around you and all the ways you are destined to continue changing the culture. Don't stop where you are. There's someone waiting for what you have. I know I am!

Confess With Me:

- I am an agent of change.
- I am full of innovative ideas.
- I am called to positively affect the culture.
- I am destined to infuse new life into things that have died.
- I am a culture changer.

Thoughts:

I'm Coming Back Strong

*"The godly may trip seven times,
but they will get up again."*
Proverbs 24:16a (NLT)

Let's be real about it, all of us have experienced some sort of setback in life. We've been faced with issues and situations that have thrown us for a loop and taken us off track for a bit. Today, I'm here to encourage you to bounce back from whatever set you back! Yes, you messed up! No it didn't work out as planned! Yes, your resources are limited (right now), but that doesn't mean that you can't try again.

The Bible declares in Proverbs chapter 24, in the first part of verse 16, that a godly man falls seven times, but he gets back up again! My friend, you may have fallen. You may have even experienced some devastating blows, but I pray that you receive strength to get back up and to come back strong! Never forget, no matter how many times you've fallen or how many times you've been knocked down, you can always get back up because the greater one lives inside of you.

Confess With Me:

- I am not defined by what WAS.
- I am not crippled by what happened.
- I have strength to try again.
- I am stepping into what IS and what WILL BE.
- I'm coming back strong.

Thoughts:

I Am A Giant Slayer

*"But you belong to God, my dear children.
You have already won a victory over those people,
because the Spirit who lives in you is greater than
the spirit who lives in the world."*

1 John 4:4 (NLT)

What is a giant? Metaphorically speaking, a giant is something that is bigger than average. It possesses massive strength and can more often than not take someone out! Giants are big, they're scary, they're intimidating and powerful. Be that as it may, I want you to know that you my friend are more powerful than even the strongest giant. You are a giant slayer. You possess within your very being the power and ability to knock down any giant that comes to destroy you! Now, when I say giant, I'm not referring to a physical being. I'm talking about systems and thoughts and ideas that seek to take you down and keep you small. Your giant may be self-doubt and insecurity while another person's giant may be overeating, lying, or complacency. The Bible tells us in 1 John chapter 4 verse 4 that the greater one lives inside of us! What does that mean? It means that if Christ lives inside of you, you cannot be defeated!

Today, stand fully in the power that you possess. Speak positively over yourself and those around you. Never forget that giants DO fall, and you have the power to bring them down.

Confess With Me:
- I fear nothing that comes against me.
- I am courageous.
- I have strategy.
- I am equipped to dismantle everything that seeks to destroy me.

Thoughts:

I Release It

"Give all your worries and cares to God, for he cares about you."
1 Peter 5:7 (NLT)

Release: allow or enable to escape from confinement; set free; allow (something) to move, act, or flow freely.

Grudges. Past hurts. Mistakes. Bad choices. How many times have we held on to these things, dragging them behind us and carrying them from place to place like precious cargo? Sometimes we carry stuff around so long until it becomes the norm, causing us not to realize how weighted down we are or how much damage is being done as a result of the weight. We carry these things so long until they become our prison, and we just reside there in quiet misery.

I was watching a television show recently, and a mother told her son, who was in prison, "You're not the only one who's in here. Your family is in here with you too." Now, on one hand that comment could mean that his family had his back and was willing to support him until he was released. On the other hand, it could mean that his family is feeling the negative effects of his choices and are suffering right along with him. How many people are being affected by the things you're holding on to?

Friend, today I invite you to do some self-examination. Look deep inside of yourself and acknowledge the things that you're holding on to. Then ask the Lord to search your heart and show you even more of what you need to release. Once you are aware of the "stuff" you're carrying you can make a conscious decision to begin to release, let go, and ultimately heal. I pray that you begin to release yourself from the past. Release every person who has ever done you wrong and watch the beauty that unfolds.

Confess With Me:
- I release myself from my past.
- I release myself from shame.
- I release myself from overwhelming expectations.
- I release all those who have hurt me.

Thoughts:

I Will Never Be Defeated

"We are pressed on every side by troubles, but we are not crushed. We are perplexed, but not driven to despair. We are hunted down, but never abandoned by God. We get knocked down, but we are not destroyed."

2 Corinthians 4:8-9 (NLT)

Everyone I know has experienced some sort of battle, and there are some battles we face that can feel overwhelming. Now, we win some and we lose some, but we are NEVER defeated. I want to let you know the difference between victory and defeat is all in your mindset. If you walk around with a negative mindset that always dwells on the worst in life, you will be defeated. However, if you shift your mindset and dwell on positive things, your entire world can change. I'm not saying that challenges and battles won't come because they will. However, when all is said and done, you choose the outcome. Even when you get knocked down, it is up to you to get up, dust yourself off and get back in the game.

Today, I want to offer you a bit of encouragement and motivation. Life is tough, but you are tougher, and the only way to win is to keep on fighting. You may be tired of fighting, but the fight, the struggle, and the hard times really do show you what you are made of and teach you valuable lessons in the process. Hold your head high, keep pushing, be strategic, keep moving and eventually you'll breakthrough right to victory. Troubles come and troubles go, but my friend, you are NEVER defeated!

Confess With Me:

- Today, I declare that life is tough, but I am tougher.
- I have the strength of will and mind to withstand any storm.
- I will not be overtaken.
- I am determined to fight and WIN.
- I will never be defeated.

Thoughts:

I Am Loved

"And I am convinced that nothing can ever separate us from God's love. Neither death nor life, neither angels nor demons, neither our fears for today nor our worries about tomorrow, not even the powers of hell can separate us from God's love."

Romans 8:38 (NLT)

During one of my morning devotional times with God, I read about God's goodness. As I read, I was reminded that God is good all the time (and not in the cliché way), and His love for us knows no bounds. Romans chapter 8 around verse 38 tells us that there is nothing that will ever separate us from the love of God. No matter what (or who) comes or goes, I will never be separated from His love. I don't know about you, but I know full well that I've done some things that could have deemed me unlovable by God, yet He still shows me His love and care on a daily basis. I've also encountered situations in life that were not my fault but left me feeling alone, uncared for, and unloved.

My friend, the fact of the matter is that people hurt us; they disappoint and leave us feeling downright crushed! However, I've learned that no matter the disappointment and hurt I've experienced from others, I am still loved. Every morning when I open my eyes, I'm reminded of the great love God has for me simply because I am alive. I often tell people that I can't do anything about what someone else does or does not do, but I have all of the control in the world over myself, my choices and my reactions. So maybe people have mishandled you in some way. There may have been situations that left you feeling alone, depressed, unwanted, and unloved. I want to take a moment to reassure you that you ARE loved by our great, big, wonderful God. He has plans for you beyond anything you can even comprehend, and yes, even your pain serves a purpose and will bring you to the goal He has for you.

Confess With Me:

- I mess up every day, but my mistakes do not outweigh the love God has for me.
- God's love for me is relentless.
- God's love for me is never failing.
- God passionately pursues me.
- God uses people to show me that I am indeed loved.

Thoughts:

My Future Awaits Me

*"For I know the plans I have for you, says the Lord.
They are plans for good and not for disaster,
to give you a future and a hope"*

Jeremiah 29:11 (NLT)

Friend, as we close out these 31 days of confessions, I want you to dig deep inside of yourself. Take the time to figure out what it is you wish to see manifested in your life? What are your goals? Your visions? Your dreams? Get a picture in your mind and let that be your focal point. Pray and ask God to reveal your purpose. On a personal note, once my purpose was revealed to me, I received so much clarity and peace. And if I'm honest, learning more about my purpose has also caused me some anxiety and stress at times, but I believe that this is all a part of the process. Learning and accepting my purpose has shown me that there is so much more that lies ahead, so I can't afford to get stuck in the present.

My friend, tap into yourself as you tap into God. I encourage you to write your goals, confess them with your mouth, and make them a part of your daily life because your future awaits you.

Confess With Me:

- I am in tune with myself and my destiny.
- I make attainable goals, and I work toward them.
- I am committed to becoming the best possible version of myself and fulfilling my destiny.

Thoughts:

My Confessions Of Faith

"Then the Lord answered me and said, "Record the vision and inscribe it on tablets, that the one who reads it may run. For the vision is yet for the appointed time; it hastens toward the goal and it will not fail. Though it tarries, wait for it; for it will certainly come, it will not delay.."

Habakkuk 2:2-3

I Confess...

1) _____

2) _____

3) _____

4) _____

5) _____

6) _____

7) _____

8) _____

9) _____

10) _____

11) _____

12) _____

13) _____

14) _____

15) _____

16) _____

17) _____

18) _____

19) _____

20) _____

21) _____

My Confessions Of Faith | 107

22) _____

23) _____

24) _____

25) _____

26) _____

27) _____

28) _____

29) _____

30) _____

31) _____

About The Author

SHAKIRA N. JONES

From a young age faith became the foundation of Shakira's world. Being raised in the inner-city in the Bronx, NY Shakira's mother kept her in church where she learned to read the Bible, pray, and have faith in God. As a child it didn't mean much, but as she grew into adulthood Shakira's faith proved to be the foundation that she needed. From professing the college she would attend, to choosing a career path, to relocating and making major moves, everything Shakira has done has been an act of faith. It is her faith that has carried her through, brought her to this point in life and allowed this book to be a reality.

Shakira is now a licensed Master of Social Work (LMSW) residing in Charleston, South Carolina where she works as an elementary school counselor.

Connect with Shakira:

Instagram: @ShakiraNicole